Till Death Do Us Part

*Encouragement for a
Grieving Spouse*

Victoria Cooper

NEW HARBOR PRESS / RAPID CITY, SD

Cooper/New Harbor Press
1601 Mt Rushmore Rd, Ste 3288
Rapid City, SD 57701
www.NewHarborPress.com

Till Death Do Us Part / Victoria Cooper. -- 1st ed.
ISBN 978-1-63357-468-7

Unless otherwise noted, Scripture quotations are taken from the Holy Bible, New International Version®, NIV®, Copyright© 1973, 1978, 1984, 2011 by Biblica, Inc ®. Used by permission. All rights reserved worldwide.

Other Scripture quotations are from the following sources: The Holy Bible, Evangelical Heritage Version®, EHV®, Copyright© 2019 Wartberg Project, Inc. All rights reserved; King James Version (KJV), Public Domain; New King James Version® (NKJV), Copyright© 1982 by Thomas Nelson. Used by permission. All rights reserved: The Message (MSG), Copyright© 1993, 2002, 2018 by Eugene H. Peterson

Hymns listed are in public domain

I dedicate this book to my mother, who assured me that God would be with me through my grief and bring me out whole.

I also dedicate it to all who know the pain of a spouse's transition and look to God for strength and guidance.

Look to the Lord and his strength; seek his face always. 1 Chronicles 16:11

In the morning, Lord, you hear my voice; in the morning I lay my requests before you and wait expectantly. Psalm 5:3

Those who know your name trust in you, for you, Lord, have never forsaken those who seek you. Psalm 9:10

Contents

Acknowledgments

Thank you to all who have heard me talk about this collection over many years. To my sister, Dr. Elaine Woodson, Ed.D for her review and suggestions. To those women and men I've encountered over the years who shared their grief and allowed the Lord to give me another word of encouragement. I am thankful for all of you.

Introduction

When my second husband transitioned, ten years after my first, I was devastated and grief stricken. I had fasted, prayed and believed in his full recovery, and was convinced that his steady progress was confirmation that our specific prayer was being answered. His transition, a few weeks after a major setback, shook me to my core and for awhile I questioned whether I had prayed enough or genuinely believed my prayers. I began to document my feelings and thoughts from day to day. This enabled a comparison of my feelings with the Truth in Scriptures. In every instance, Scripture took my mind away from my grief and focused it on God. His goodness, His faithfulness, His Omnipresence, His Omnipotence, His Love, His trustworthiness, His ability to Comfort, and the knowledge that He has never failed me.

I also began to document discussions with others on their journey of grieving and mourning a spouse. There are differences between spousal grief and other types of grief. In marriage, God created a mystery, the oneness of two people. The two become one, not only through children but with each other. When a spouse transitions, a part of us has left. God knows this and He knows what is required to fill that void.

These encouragements were written over a nine-year period, as I experienced various thoughts, feelings, and emotions, and encountered those of others.

Each encouragement is written in the first person, as these may be feelings and thoughts you have or have had. Each encouragement also includes affirmations to help you get through those feelings, deal with the emotions, and reflect on what you know and believe about God and His Word. There are scriptures that support the encouragement; these can be memorized and used to stand on, as they are the Word of God. His Word does not fail.

A hymn ends each encouragement. These can take you through the day or night. If you don't know the tunes, find them in a hymnal or online and allow them to minister to your soul.

After each encouragement, pause and reflect on your feelings, the reading, the scriptures, and the hymn. Find what they say to you and what God says to you, through them. These are not meant to be read in one sitting.

My prayer is that these encouragements comfort you on this journey and provide the assurance that our God loves you, is with you, and will never leave you or forsake you. He can be trusted.

Be Blessed

Victoria Cooper

It's a New Journey

You may have picked up this book to try to make sense of what has happened, or to begin to cope with it. That's a good thing, because the grieving and mourning process requires deliberate intention.

If you are still feeling numb, give yourself some time. Just remember to trust the truth in the Word of God.

2 Corinthians 12:9 My grace is sufficient for you, for my power is made perfect in weakness.

Deuteronomy 33:25 (KJV) as thy days, so shall thy strength be.

Psalm 23:3 (NKJV) He restores my soul.

For now, trust Him to completely uphold you. When you have a little strength, He will help you along and when the pain lessens, He will strengthen you as needed.

When you are ready, move through the encouragements, embrace the scriptures, and sing the hymns. In time you'll be able to smile at the memories without crying. Allow the Holy Spirit, the Comforter, to do His work. He will take you through.

Psalm 31:14-15 But I trust in you, Lord; I say "You are my God." My times are in your hands.

Psalm 34:17-18 The righteous cry out, and the Lord hears them; he delivers them from all their troubles. The Lord is close to the broken hearted and saves those who are crushed in spirit.

Psalm 42:5 Why, my soul, are you downcast? Why so disturbed within me? Put your hope in God, for I will yet praise Him, my Savior and my God.

Isaiah 41:10 So do not fear, for I am with you; do not be dismayed, for I am your God. I will strengthen you and help you; I will uphold you with my righteous right hand.

Psalm 42:1-10 (MSG)
A white-tailed deer drinks from the creek; I want to drink God, deep drafts of God. I'm thirsty for God-alive. I wonder, "Will I ever make it—arrive and drink in God's presence?" I'm on a diet of tears—tears for breakfast, tears for supper. All day long people knock at my door, Pestering, "Where is this God of yours?"

These are the things I go over and over, emptying out the pockets of my life. I was always at the head of the worshiping crowd, right out in front, leading them all, eager to arrive and worship, Shouting praises, singing thanksgiving— celebrating, all of us, God's feast! Why are you down in the dumps, dear soul? Why are you crying the blues?

Fix my eyes on God—soon I'll be praising again. He puts a smile on my face. He's my God.

When my soul is in the dumps, I rehearse everything I know of you, From Jordan depths to Hermon heights, including Mount Mizar. Chaos calls to chaos, to the tune of whitewater rapids. Your breaking surf, your thundering breakers crash and crush me. Then God promises to love me all day, sing songs all through the night! My life is God's prayer. Sometimes I ask God, my rock-solid God, "Why did you let me down? Why am I walking around in tears, harassed by enemies?" They're out for the kill, these tormentors with their obscenities, Taunting day after day, "Where is this God of yours?"

Reflection

1

The Strength I Need, I Have

There are days when it takes every ounce of strength to get out of bed and face the day. My mind is telling me to put on a strong face for children, family, friends, work, and all manner of "others" because I have always been strong or that is what I "should" do. I cannot show my vulnerability, so I smile to keep up appearances, while it feels like a knife is cutting through my very soul. Amid all this, it is easy to forget God's promises, but I must not. I know and believe the strength I need is in Him alone. Each time I wake up, morning or night, I must draw on the strength of the Holy Spirit in me. I lean on Jesus; He knows me thoroughly and He will get me through this. I Trust Him. I will not worry about what this day will bring, or tomorrow, or how I will make it through this or that. He gives me the strength I need for today, and He will do the same for tomorrow. He has it all under control, my strength is not required.

Psalm 59:16-17 But I will sing of your strength, in the morning I will sing of your love; for you are my fortress, my refuge in times of trouble. You are my strength, I sing praise to you; you, God, are my fortress, my God on whom I can rely.

2 Corinthians 12:9 (KJV) And he said unto me, My grace is sufficient for thee: for my strength is made perfect in weakness. Most gladly therefore will I rather glory in my infirmities, that the power of Christ may rest upon me.

Deuteronomy 33:25b (KJV) As thy days, so shall thy strength be.

I Will Go in the Strength of the Lord
(Edward Turney)

I will go in the strength of the Lord, In the path He hath marked for my feet; I will follow the light of His word, Nor shrink from the dangers I meet. His presence my steps shall attend; His fullness my wants shall supply; On Him, till my journey shall end, My hope shall securely rely.

I will go in the strength of the Lord To the work He appoints me to do: In the joy which His smile shall afford, My soul shall her vigor renew, His wisdom will guard me from harm His power, my sufficiency prove; I will trust His omnipotent arm, I will rest in His covenant love.

I will go in the strength of the Lord, To each conflict which faith may require; His grace, as my shield and reward, My courage and zeal shall inspire, If He issue the word of command To meet and encounter the foe, Though with sling and with stone in my hand, In the strength of the Lord, I will go.

Reflection

2

God Is Enough

They are not with me anymore. I don't know what to do. I don't know how to do anything and I don't feel like doing anything. I don't want to go on without them. I only want to cover my head until all this goes away. I want a hug; I want to hold them and tell them "I love you" once more. I want some peace but it's hard to find right now. It's all dark, I'm tired of feeling this way, and this feeling won't go away. When I think about the love of Jesus, I feel calm in His presence. I inhale deeply and exhale slowly. I know and believe the Holy Spirit will help me internalize that God's love is enough, His peace is enough, and His grace is enough. I will hold onto these truths until I'm stronger.

Psalm 90:2 Before the mountains were born or you brought forth the whole world, from everlasting to everlasting you are God.

Exodus 3:14 God said to Moses, "I am who I am. This is what you are to say to the Israelites: 'I am has sent me to you.'"

Isaiah 41:13 For I am the Lord, your God who takes hold of your right hand and says to you, Do not fear; I will help you.

Zephaniah 3:17 (EHV) The Lord your God is with you as a hero who will save you. He takes great delight in you. He will quiet you with his love. He will rejoice over you with singing."

Habakkuk 3:17-18 Though the fig tree does not bud and there are no grapes on the vines, though the olive crop fails and the fields produce no food, though there are no sheep in the pen and no cattle in the stalls, yet I will rejoice in the Lord, I will be joyful in God my Savior.

I Could Not Do Without Thee
(Frances R. Havergal)

I could not do without Thee, O Savior of the lost, whose precious Blood redeemed me at such tremendous cost; Thy righteousness, Thy pardon, Thy precious Blood must be, my only hope and comfort, my glory and my plea.

I could not do without Thee, I cannot stand alone, I have no strength or goodness, no wisdom of my own; but Thou, beloved Savior art all in all to me, and weakness will be power if leaning hard on Thee.

I could not do without Thee for, oh, the way is long, and I am often weary, and sigh replaces song; How could I do without Thee? I do not know the way; Thou knowest, and Thou leadest, and wilt not let me stray.

I could not do without Thee, O Jesus, Savior dear; even when my eyes are holden I know that Thou art near; how dreary and how lonely this changeful life would be without the sweet communion, the secret rest with Thee.

I could not do without Thee, no other friend can read the spirit's strange deep longings, interpreting its need; no human heart could enter each dim recess of mine and soothe and hush and calm it, O Blessed Lord, but Thine.

I could not do without Thee for years are fleeting fast, and soon in solemn loneness the river must be passed; but Thou wilt never leave me and though the waves roll high, I know Thou wilt be near me, and whisper, "It is I."

Reflection

3

I'm Not Alone

When I come home everything is different. People may be around, and I behave as if I am adjusting to the new reality, giving the appearance that I am going on with life. When I go into our bedroom, it all changes. We lived in the room together and I can still smell them. I see the things they touched, and their presence is still there. But they are not physically there, the room is empty, and I am alone. No one knows how this feels and there are no words to describe it. So many private things were said and done in this space and we are the only ones who knew them. These are not to be shared, with anyone. So I just savor them and sit and think about them and cry. Then I speak to God who was always present and knows all the secrets, so I can speak openly. Every issue, every anxiety, every feeling of loneliness and desire for companionship, I can share with Him. I know and believe there is no valley so deep and no pit so dark that God can't see me, even if I'm on the bottom. God has been with me all along and is my constant companion. When I speak to the Lord, humbly and honestly, He speaks back through the Holy Spirit who lives in me. This changes everything, every time. I then no longer feel alone, because my friend Jesus is with me. I become more relaxed and sleep peacefully, as He gives sweet sleep. If I must do this daily, I will.

Psalm 139:7-12 Where can I go from your Spirit? Where can I flee from your presence? If I go up to the heavens, you are there; if I make my bed in the depths, you are there. If I rise on the wings of the dawn, if I settle on the far side of the sea, even there your hand will guide me, your right hand will hold me fast. If I say, "Surely the darkness will hide me and the light become night around me," even the darkness will not be dark to you; the night will shine like the day, for darkness is as light to you.

Genesis 16:13 She gave this name to the Lord who spoke to her: "You are the God who sees me," for she said, "I have now seen the One who sees me."

Joshua 1:5 No one will be able to stand against you all the days of your life. As I was with Moses, so I will be with you; I will never leave you nor forsake you.

Never Alone
(Ludie Carrington Day Pickett)

I've seen the lightning flashing and heard the thunder roll, I've felt sin's breakers dashing, trying to conquer my soul; I've heard the voice of Jesus, telling me still to fight on, He promised never to leave me, never to leave me alone.

The world's fierce winds are blowing, temptations are sharp and keen; I feel a peace in knowing, my Savior stands between; He stands to shield me from danger, when earthly friends are gone, He promised never to leave me, never to leave me alone.

When in affliction's valley, I'm treading the road of care, my Savior helps me to carry, my cross when heavy to bear; my feet entangled with briars ready to cast me down; My Savior whispered His promise, never to leave me alone.

He died for me on the mountain, for me they pierced His side, for me He opened that fountain, the crimson cleansing tide; for me He waiteth in glory, seated upon His throne; He promised never to leave me, never to leave me alone.

No, never alone, no, never alone, He promised never to leave me, never to leave me alone; no, never alone, no, never alone, He promised never to leave me, never to leave me alone.

Reflection

4

I Must Be Easy on Myself

They are not here, yet 24 hours of the day continue to roll on. I must sleep, wake and perform all the task required of me in my various roles. This is not a familiar place, there is no playbook, and I don't have answers to the questions asked about what I will do now and what's next. I am still working through the thoughts and feelings of life without them. This is very difficult, and people expect answers when I don't have them. I am barely holding it all together. All I know is that I will allow God to transition me from what He has done in my life to what He is doing in my life. I am His and He knows. I know and believe I don't have to be strong because He is. The time-line and the process are His, I don't know what it will look like, I will not force it or allow others to pressure me into decisions or actions for which I'm not ready. I will be easy on myself and intentionally give myself the time I need to grieve and mourn, allowing the Lord to strengthen me. Each day I will honestly present my mental, physical, and spiritual state to the Lord, following His instructions for the day and expecting His joy, even when I can't smile. His joy will help me think His thoughts.

Psalm 143:8 Let the morning bring me word of your unfailing love, for I have put my trust in you. Show me the way I should go, for to you I entrust my life.

Lamentations 3:22-23 Because of the Lord's great love we are not consumed, for his compassions never fail. They are new every morning; great is your faithfulness.

Nehemiah 8:10 Do not grieve, for the joy of the Lord is your strength.

I Heard the Voice of Jesus Say
(Horatius Bonar)

I heard the voice of Jesus say, "Come unto Me and rest; Lay down, thou weary one, lay down Thy head upon My breast;" I came to Jesus as I was, weary, and worn, and sad; I found in Him a resting place, and He has made me glad.

I heard the voice of Jesus say, "Behold, I freely give, the living water, thirsty one, stoop down and drink and live." I came to Jesus, and I drank of that life-giving stream: my thirst was quenched, my soul revived and now I live in Him.

I heard the voice of Jesus say, "I am this dark world's Light; Look unto Me, thy morn shall rise, and all thy day be bright:" I looked to Jesus, and I found in Him my Star, my Sun; And in that Light of life I'll walk, till travelling days are done.

Reflection

5

I Will Make It Through This

I really don't know how I will get through this. Sometimes I feel like it's okay and I'll make it, then I start pacing again trying to figure things out. It is so much. I know I should be strong; I should take charge and go ahead to get things done. But I have no energy to do anything. This is grief, this is normal, I must give it some time, but I will not let it consume me. I know and believe the Lord will help me manage it and each day I will look toward God and not at my pain. All I need to know, He knows. All I need to understand, He understands. All the challenges that must be addressed today and for which I cannot think clearly enough to sort through, He has the answer. I will deliberately lay them at the altar and give it to Him to sort out. I WILL trust Him. I will listen, to my spirit and to His guidance, it may come from an unexpected source, but I expect to hear from Him each day. My spirit will know when the word is from Him, it will be that knowing. I Trust Him.

Psalm 5:3 In the morning, Lord, you hear my voice; in the morning I lay my requests before you and wait expectantly.

John 10:27 My sheep listen to my voice; I know them, and they follow me.

Isaiah 30:21 Whether you turn to the right or to the left, your ears will hear a voice behind you, saying, "This is the way; walk in it."

2 Chronicles 20:12-17

Our God, will you not judge them? For we have no power to face this vast army that is attacking us. We do not know what to do, but our eyes are on you. All the men of Judah, with their wives and children and little ones, stood there before the Lord. Then the Spirit of the Lord came on Jahaziel son of Zechariah, the son of Benaiah, the son of Jeiel, the son of Mattaniah, a Levite and descendant of Asaph, as he stood in the assembly. He said: "Listen, King Jehoshaphat and all who live in Judah and Jerusalem! This is what the Lord says to you: 'Do not be afraid or discouraged because of this vast army. For the battle is not yours, but God's. Tomorrow march down against them. They will be climbing up by the Pass of Ziz, and you will find them at the end of the gorge in the Desert of Jeruel. You will not have to fight this battle. Take up your positions; stand firm and see the deliverance the Lord will give you, Judah and Jerusalem. Do not be afraid; do not be discouraged. Go out to face them tomorrow, and the Lord will be with you.'

Great Is Thy Faithfulness
(William M. Runyan / Thomas O Chisholm / Eric Allyn Schrotenboer)

Great is Thy faithfulness, O God my Father, there is no shadow of turning with Thee, Thou changest not, Thy compassions, they fail not as Thou hast been, Thou forever will be.

Summer and winter and springtime and harvest, sun, moon and stars in their courses above; join with all nature in manifold witness to Thy great faithfulness, mercy and love.

Pardon for sin and a peace that endureth, thine own dear presence to cheer and to guide; strength for today and bright hope for tomorrow, blessings all mine with ten thousand beside.

Great is Thy faithfulness, Great is Thy faithfulness; morning by morning new mercies I see, all I have needed Thy hand hath provided, Great is Thy faithfulness, Lord, unto me.

Reflection

6

Hold Him Tighter

There are times when I wish I could close my eyes and open them, and all this would be different. But no matter how hard I try, it doesn't change. If the world could stop for just a few days to allow me to absorb all that is happening and adjust, maybe I could handle this better, but it doesn't stop for me. It may seem like things are falling apart and they may, in fact, be falling apart, but God is in control. I know and believe He is within me; I will not fall! When I close my eyes, I will fix my thoughts and eyes on Christ. I will focus on His love, saying, "I Trust You Jesus" as a constant mantra. I will hold Jesus tighter. He will never leave me or forsake me.

Psalm 46:1-5 God is our refuge and strength, an ever-present help in trouble, Therefore, we will not fear, though the earth give way and the mountains fall into the heart of the sea, though its waters roar and foam and the mountains quake with their surging. There is a river whose streams make glad the city of God, the holy place where the

Most High dwells. God is within her, she will not fall; God will help her at break of day.

Deuteronomy 31:8 The Lord himself goes before you and will be with you; he will never leave you nor forsake you. Do not be afraid; do not be discouraged.

Jesu, Lover of my Soul
(Rev. Charles Wesley)

Jesu, Lover of my soul, let me to Thy Bosom fly, While the gathering waters roll, while the tempest still is high: Hide me, O my Savior, hide, till the storm of life is past; Safe into the haven guide, O receive my soul at last.

Other refuge have I none, hangs my helpless soul on Thee; Leave ah! Leave me not alone, still support and comfort me. All my trust on Thee is stayed, all my help from Thee I bring; Cover my defenseless head, with the shelter of Thy wing.

Plenteous grace with Thee is found, grace to cleanse from every sin; Let the healing streams abound, make and keep me pure within; Thou of Life the Fountain art, freely let me take of Thee; Spring Thou up within my heart rise to all eternity.

Reflection

7

I Overcome by My Testimony

I really don't want to keep telling people what happened or how I feel. I don't want to break that awkward silence when well-meaning friends and loved ones ask the question. Each time I tell the story it requires me to go back to that moment, the thoughts and emotions that I must accept and somehow manage. The truth of their absence is difficult; speaking that truth over and over somehow seems to help me accept it, although I don't like to do it. Speaking the truth of my sadness opens the door to the truth of joyful times together, and in fact brings them back to life in my heart. Although tears may fall when sharing the story of their transition, it allows me to begin to think of moments that made me smile. So speaking will bring me to a better place and move those thoughts that should not linger. I know and believe, there are many others, particularly within the household of faith, who have traversed this journey, I can speak to them. We overcome by our testimony and that of others.

Psalm 71:15 My mouth will tell of your righteous deeds, of your saving acts all day long—though I know not how to relate them all.

Psalm 40:10 I do not hide your righteousness in my heart; I speak of your faithfulness and your saving help. I do not conceal your love and your faithfulness from the great assembly.

Revelation 12:11 They triumphed over him by the blood of the Lamb and by the word of their testimony; they did not love their lives so much as to shrink from death.

Praise to the Lord, the Almighty
(Joachim Neander)

Praise to the Lord, the Almighty, the King of creation; O my soul, praise Him, for He is thy health and salvation; All ye who hear, Now to His temple draw near, Joining in glad adoration.

Praise to the Lord, Who over all things so wondrously reigneth, Shieldeth thee gently from harm or when fainting sustaineth; Hast though not seen, how thy heart's wishes have been, Granted in what he ordaineth?

Praise to the Lord, Who doeth prosper thy work and defend thee, Surely His goodness and mercy shall daily attend thee; Ponder anew what the Almighty can do, If to the end He befriend thee.

Reflection

8

There Is Light in That Dark Place

Life's transition and its finality permeate almost every thought. The pain of this experience and thoughts of my eventual mortality are ever present. Sometimes I sink into the darkness as there is no light to be found. I wonder if I can make it alone, without them. With all these thoughts, I must, and I will Trust You Jesus. I will not give up. Although this is a dark place, I know and believe the light of Jesus shines here, even when I don't see it. Although I don't see it or feel it, I KNOW you are with me because your Word is true. The darkness will not hold me here and depression will not settle in. Thank you, Lord, for bringing light into my dark place. Where you are, there is no darkness at all. Yes, this is dark, yes, it is difficult, yes I will grieve, yes I will mourn, but I will not allow my thoughts to keep me from your Light and the plans you still have for me in this life. I will keep my eyes on you and the warmth of your Light will make each day brighter.

Psalm 40:2-3 He lifted me out of the slimy pit, out of the mud and mire; he set my feet on a rock and gave me a firm place to stand. He put a new song in my mouth, a hymn of praise to our God. Many will see and fear the Lord and put their trust in him.

Isaiah 42:16 I will lead the blind by ways they have not known; along unfamiliar paths I will guide them; I will turn the darkness into light before them and make the rough places smooth. These are the things I will do; I will not forsake them.

2 Corinthians 10:5 We demolish arguments and every pretension that sets itself up against the knowledge of God, and we take captive every thought to make it obedient to Christ.

Philippians 4:8 Finally, brothers and sisters, whatever is true, whatever is noble, whatever is right, whatever is pure, whatever is lovely, whatever is admirable—if anything is excellent or praiseworthy— think about such things.

Give Light O Lord
(Lawrence Tuttiett)

Give light, O Lord that we may learn the way that leads to Thee, that where our hearts true joys discern our life may be.

Give light, O Lord, that we may know Thy one unchanging truth, and follow all our days below, our Guide in youth.

Give light, O Lord, that we may see where wisdom bids beware, and turn our doubting minds to Thee in faithful prayer.

Give light, O Lord, that we may look beneath, around, above, and learn from nature's living book Thy power and love.

Give light, O Lord, that we may read all signs that Thou art near, And, while we live in word and deed Thy name revere.

Give light, O Lord, that we may trace in trial, pain and loss, in poorest lot, and lowest place a Savior's Cross.

Give light, O Lord, that we may see a home beyond the sky, where all who live in Christ with Thee shall never die.

Reflection

9

The Lord Will Carry the Load

Dealing with everything feels like it is just too much to carry. It's a lot and I'm trying to get through it. The issues keep coming, things I know and things I know nothing about, but must manage. Part of the anxiety is that I don't know what will be thrown my way tomorrow. Some issues are complex, and I'll need help but I don't know where to turn to get it. One thing I know, if I try to carry it alone, it can crush me, so I will give it to Jesus. I know He said His yoke was easy and His burden was light, so I believe Him. Nothing in my life is coincidence. It may have been unexpected, but I am more prepared than I realize. This burden is from Him, if it feels heavy, I will stop looking at it and look at Him. I'll take a few minutes to quiet my mind and spirit and sit in His presence. The weight will lift, and my mind will clear enough to continue to stand firm or take the next step.

Psalm 55:22 Cast your cares on the Lord and he will sustain you; he will never let the righteous be shaken.

Matthew 11:28-30 "Come to me, all you who are weary and burdened, and I will give you rest. Take my yoke upon you and learn from me, for I am gentle and humble in heart, and you will find rest for your souls. For my yoke is easy and my burden is light."

Isaiah 41:13 For I am the Lord your God who takes hold of your right hand and says to you, Do not fear; I will help you.

1 Peter 5:6-7 Humble yourselves, therefore, under God's mighty hand, that he may lift you up in due time. Cast all your anxiety on him because he cares for you.

How Sweet the Name of Jesus Sounds
(John Newton)

How sweet the Name of Jesus sounds in a believer's ear! It soothes his sorrows, heals his wounds, and drives away the fear.

It makes the wounded spirit whole and calms the troubled breast; 'Tis manna to the hungry soul, and to the weary rest.

Dear Name, the rock on which I build, my shield and hiding place, my never-failing treasury filled with boundless stores of grace.

Jesus! My Shepherd, Husband, Friend, My Prophet, Priest, and King, My Lord, my Life, my Way, my End, accept the praise I bring.

Weak is the effort of my heart, and cold my warmest thought; But when I see Thee as Thou art, I'll praise Thee as I ought.

Till then I would Thy love proclaim with every fleeting breath; And may the music of Thy Name refresh my soul in death.

Reflection

10

The Fog Will Lift

It takes so much effort to make simple decisions; I seem to be unsure of everything. Their absence has changed all that I do, including the way I process information. I could always assess a situation, decide actions, and take charge to get it done. Not now, everything is cloudy, it is like a dream, and nothing seems real. It's difficult to process what has happened and its implications, to enable decisions to be made. All I know and believe is that God is in control. All I know and believe is that He is the same yesterday, today, and forever. All I know and believe is I will hold Him tighter and ask Him for guidance for today. He will take care of tomorrow when it comes, because I cannot see or even think that far with this fog in my head. People who were on this journey before me, assure me it will lift. So, I simply trust God. I have noticed that I have more clarity when I am closer to Him, therefore, I will follow Jesus' voice as he guides me step by step, day by day. I will trust His process. I will continually go to the Lord for guidance on simple, mundane things, and decision making won't seem so onerous. I will increase my trust in Him and the fog will lift, maybe slowly, but it will lift. I await the morning I wake up and realize that I am so confident in His daily guidance that there is no fog. For now, I will trust Him.

Psalm 32:8 I will instruct you and teach you in the way you should go; I will counsel you with my loving eye on you.

Isaiah 30:20-21 Although the Lord gives you the bread of adversity and water of affliction, your teachers will be hidden no more, with your own eyes you will see them. Whether you turn to the right or to the left, your ears will hear a voice behind you saying, "This is the way; walk in it."

Isaiah 41:10 So do not fear, for I am with you; do not be dismayed, for I am your God. I will strengthen you and help you; I will uphold you with my righteous right hand.

Psalm 13:5-6 But I trust in your unfailing love; my heart rejoices in your salvation. I will sing the Lord's praise, for he has been good to me.

Through All the Changing Scenes of Life
(Nahum Tate)

Through all the changing scenes of life, in trouble and in joy, The praises of my God shall still my heart and tongue employ.

O magnify the Lord with me, with me exalt His Name; When in distress to Him I called, He to my rescue came.

The Hosts of God encamp around the dwellings of the just; Deliverance He affords to all who on His succor trust.

O make but trial of His love, experience will decide. How blessed are they, and only they who in His truth confide.

Fear Him, ye saints and you will then, have nothing else to fear; Make you His service your delight, your wants will be his care.

Reflection

11

I Will Stand Still and Know

I need a word from the Lord. It seems like He is quiet and that I must go on. I don't want to go in the wrong direction and it's difficult to make decisions on what to do. The real issue is that I don't know what I even want to do. So, my best move is no move at all. I will stay prayerful and seek the Lord's face until I hear from Him. I won't stop and sit at home, but I will keep my mind on Him for His direction in small and big decisions I must make. I won't try to consider them in advance; if I need to make a quick decision, the Lord knows and will give me an immediate response. I know and believe He is Omnipresent. He knows my name and He knows my needs. When He says, "Be Still and Know," He wants me to still my thoughts and not be anxious about things around me. I can continue to do many things, but my spirit will be still, waiting to hear from Him. This is the best move I can make. The tears may flow, I will continue to hold to His unchanging hand. He is the same yesterday, today, and forever.

Psalm 46:10 He says, "Be still, and know that I am God; I will be exalted among the nations, I will be exalted in the earth.

Ephesians 6:10-13 Finally, be strong in the Lord and in his mighty power. Put on the full armor of God, so that you can take your stand against the devil's schemes. For our struggle is not against flesh and blood, but against the rulers, against the authorities, against the powers of this dark world and against the spiritual forces of evil in the heavenly realms. Therefore put on the full armor of God, so that when the day of evil comes, you may be able to stand your ground, and after you have done everything, to stand.

Jeremiah 29:10-11 This is what the Lord says: "When seventy years are completed for Babylon, I will come to you and fulfill my good promise to bring you back to this place. For I know the plans I have for you," declares the Lord, "plans to prosper you and not to harm you, plans to give you hope and a future.

Master, Speak
(Frances Ridley Havergal)

Master speak, thy servant hearth, waiting for Thy gracious word, longing for Thy voice that cheereth, Master, let it now be heard. I am listening, Lord, for Thee, what hast Thou to say to me.

Often though my heart is pealing, many another voice than Thine, many an unwilled echo stealing, from the walls of this Thy shrine, let Thy longed for accents fall, Master speak, and silence all.

Master speak, and make me ready, when Thy voice is truly heard, with obedience glad and steady, still to follow every word, I am listening, Lord for Thee, Master speak, oh, speak to me.

Speak to me by name, O Master, let me know it is to me. Speak that I may follow faster with a step more firm and free, where the shepherd leads the flock, in the shadow of the rock.

Reflection

12

He Knows and Understands

I wish I could understand what happened and what is happening. I continue to go over everything in my mind, is there something I could have done, is there something I did, what would have happened if this or that was done or was available. Is there something I am supposed to learn from this? What is God doing in my life right now? Why at this time? With all that is going on, I want to understand but no matter how hard I try, I don't. Others come and give their ideas as to why, but none of that helps me. It's like God is silent with this answer. I know and believe I should trust God when I don't understand, so I will. Each time my thoughts start trying to figure this out, I will say 'I trust you Jesus, I know You know, please give me the strength to trust you more.'

Psalm 100:3 Know that the Lord is God. It is he who made us, and we are his; we are his people, the sheep of his pasture.

Psalm 147:4-5 He determines the number of the stars and calls them each by name. Great is our Lord and mighty in power; his understanding has no limit.

Proverbs 3:5-6 Trust in the Lord with all your heart and lean not on your own understanding; in all your ways submit to him, and he will make your paths straight.

Isaiah 46:3-4 Listen to me, you descendants of Jacob, all the remnant of the people of Israel, you whom I have upheld since your birth, and have carried since you were born. Even to your old age and gray hairs I am he, I am he who will sustain you. I have made you and I will carry you; I will sustain you and I will rescue you.

Thou, Lord, by strictest search has known
(Nahum Tate)

Thou, Lord, by strictest search has known, my rising up and lying down; My secret thoughts are known to Thee, known long before conceived by me.

Thine eye my bed and path surveys, my public haunts and private ways; Though knowest what 'tis my lips would vent, my yet unuttered word's intent.

Surrounded by Thy power I stand on every side I find Thy hand, O skill, for human reach too high! Too dazzling bright for mortal eye!

Search, try, O God, my thought and heart, if mischief lurks in any part, correct me where I go astray and guide me in Thy perfect way.

Reflection

13

I Take It to Jesus

There are so many things no one else knows or will know. There are things I can't share with anyone. I think about them and smile or cry, they were ours. I will hold these in my heart. Jesus knows everything and He is my friend, I can share all my good and bad memories with Him, without explanation. Maybe some of them I'll share with friends and family, but not all, those were ours. Good or bad. I will take everything to the Lord, He is my confidant, and my joy is in Him. I know and believe the joy of the Lord IS my strength.

Psalm 13:5-6 But I trust in your unfailing love; my heart rejoices in your salvation. I will sing the Lord's praise, for he has been good to me.

Matthew 11:28-30 Come to me, all you who are weary and burdened, and I will give you rest. Take my yoke upon you and learn from me, for I am gentle and humble in heart, and you will find rest for your souls. For my yoke is easy and my burden is light.

Nehemiah 8:10 Do not grieve, for the joy of the Lord is your strength.

I Must Tell Jesus
(E. A. Hoffman)

I must tell Jesus all of my trials, I cannot bear these burdens alone, in my distress He kindly will help me, He ever loves and cares for His own.

I must tell Jesus all of my troubles; He is a kind compassionate friend, If I but ask Him, He will deliver, make of my troubles quickly an end.

Tempted and tried, I need a great Savior, one who can help my burden to bear; I must tell Jesus, I must tell Jesus, He all my cares and sorrows will share.

O how the world to evil allures me! O how my heart is tempted to sin! I must tell Jesus, and He will help me over the world the victory to win.

I must tell Jesus! I must tell Jesus! I cannot bear my burdens alone; I must tell Jesus! I must tell Jesus! Jesus can help me, Jesus alone.

Reflection

14

He Has Not Forgotten Me

It seems as though the Lord has gone quiet sometimes. I can't hear Him, maybe He has forgotten about me and all that I'm going through. I am so firm in my faith, but this is different. I've never been in a place like this spiritually, it really feels like I'm alone. When Elisah was in the desert the Lord found him in that place, so He knows where I am, but I can't feel it. I will not trust my feelings or emotions, they are real, but they are not the truth. I know and believe Jesus and the Word of God are the truth. I will keep the truth of his presence and his love ever before me, because it is the truth. This is a journey and I trust TRUTH.

Psalm 94:18-19 When I said, "My foot is slipping," your unfailing love, Lord, supported me. When anxiety was great within me, your consolation brought me joy.

Isaiah 49:15-16 Can a mother forget the baby at her breast and have no compassion on the child she has borne? Though she may forget,

I will not forget you! See, I have engraved you on the palms of my hands; your walls are ever before me.

John 14:6 Jesus answered, "I am the way and the truth and the life. No one comes to the Father except through me."

Luke 15:4-6 Suppose one of you has a hundred sheep and loses one of them. Doesn't he leave the ninety-nine in the open country and go after the lost sheep until he finds it? And when he finds it, he joyfully puts it on his shoulders and goes home. Then he calls his friends and neighbors together and says, 'Rejoice with me; I have found my lost sheep.'

Hark, My Soul! It is the Lord
(William Cowper)

Hark, my soul! It is the Lord; 'Tis thy Savior, hear His Word, Jesus speaks, and speaks to thee, "Say, poor sinner, lovest thou me?"

"I delivered thee when bound, and, when bleeding healed thy wound; Sought thee wandering, set thee right, turned thy darkness into light.

"Can a woman's tender care cease towards the child she bear? Yes, she may forgetful be, yet will I remember thee.

"Mine is an unchanging love, higher than the heights above, Deeper than the depths beneath, free and faithful, strong as death.

"Though shalt see My glory soon, When the work of grace is done; Partner of My Throne shalt be; Say, poor sinner, lovest though me?

"Lord, it is my chief complaint that my love is weak and faint; Yet I love Thee and adore, O for grace to love Thee more.

Reflection

15

Love Covers a Multitude of Sins

It's difficult to explain why I hurt so much, when I think of all the terrible things they did. My emotions are all over the place. I am sad, angry, ashamed of what they did and at times I can't say anything when people remind me of the wrongs. I still hurt because I loved them, although disagreeing with the wrongs. Sometimes I am almost relieved they are gone, other times wishing I could know they had at least reconciled with Jesus before going, other times regretting the hurtful words on both sides, other times wondering if there was more I could have done to change them or me or if I was the cause of it. I loved a person who was bad to themselves, me or others. I find it difficult to reconcile why I would still love them, but I do. My love was sometimes unconditional and sometimes conditional, but I loved. Love overshadowed their behavior and at times was given tough, but I loved. Now they are gone. I think of my Lord Jesus who loved me so much He died for me, when I did not deserve to be loved. Jesus received a thief into paradise with Him during his last hours on the cross. What my love's last spiritual seconds were, I will never know, but I know and believe Jesus saves. I will not apologize for loving them and grieving them, although I regret their wrongs and apologize to those they hurt and seek forgiveness from them, including myself. Christ loved and died for bad people.

Psalm 103:9-12 He will not always accuse, nor will he harbor his anger forever; he does not treat us as our sins deserve or repay us according to our iniquities. For as high as the heavens are above the earth, so great is his love for those who fear him; as far as the east is from the west, so far has he removed our transgressions from us.

1 Corinthians 13:8 Love never fails.

1 Peter 4:8 Above all, love each other deeply, because love covers over a multitude of sins.

Romans 5:8 But God demonstrates his own love for us in this: While we were still sinners, Christ died for us.

Luke 23:40-43 But the other criminal rebuked him. "Don't you fear God," he said, "since you are under the same sentence? We are punished justly, for we are getting what our deeds deserve. But this man has done nothing wrong." Then he said, "Jesus, remember me when you come into your kingdom." Jesus answered him, "Truly I tell you, today you will be with me in paradise."

There Is a Fountain Filled with Blood
(William Cowper)

*There is a fountain filled with blood, drawn from Immanuel's veins;
and sinners plunged beneath that flood, lose all their guilty stains,
lose all their guilty stains, lose all their guilty stains, and sinners,
plunged beneath that flood, lose all their guilty stains.*

*The dying thief rejoiced to see that fountain in his day; and there may
I, though vile as he, wash all my sins away, wash all my sins away,
wash all my sins away; and there may I, though vile as he, wash all
my sins away.*

*Dear dying Lamb, Thy precious blood shall never lose its power, till
all the ransomed Church of God be saved, to sin no more, be saved, to
sin no more, be saved to sin no more; till all the ransomed Church of
God be saved to sin no more.*

*Ever since by faith I saw that stream, Thy flowing wounds supply,
redeeming love has been my theme and shall be till I die, and shall
be till I die, and shall be till I die, redeeming love has been my theme
and shall be till I die.*

Reflection

16

He Is a Provider

This happened with no planning, and it was totally unexpected. I don't know how I'll make it with the children, expenses, the house issues, being alone, all of it. This seems so overwhelming. Things I don't know how to do or never knew about or how to handle must get done. I don't know what to do or who to trust. My head is spinning. As I rub my forehead, the Holy Spirit reminds me that I serve a God who controls everything and knows everything. Most importantly, He loves me, cares for me, and has not left me. I will quiet my thoughts and open my eyes, ears, and heart to see Him and hear from Him. I know and believe He is my Shepherd, and His voice will guide me to all that I need, exactly when it's needed. I'll keep calm and listen for His voice because it gives peace in this storm. I will know, in my spirit, when God is speaking although the words and provision sometimes come from unlikely sources. He knows what I need, when I need it and where it is. I trust you Jesus.

Psalm 145:15-16 The eyes of all look to you, and you give them their food at the proper time. You open your hand and satisfy the desires of every living thing.

Philippians 4:19 And my God will meet all your needs according to the riches of his glory in Christ Jesus.

Isaiah 43:19 See, I am doing a new thing! Now it springs up; do you not perceive it? I am making a way in the wilderness and streams in the wasteland.

Isaiah 58:11 The Lord will guide you always; he will satisfy your needs in a sun-scorched land and will strengthen your frame. You will be like a well-watered garden, like a spring whose waters never fail.

Take Not Thought for Food or Raiment
Unknown

Take not thought for food or raiment, careful one, so anxiously; For the King Himself provideth food and clothes for thee.

He Who daily feeds the sparrows, He Who clothes the lilies bright. More than birds and flowers holds thee, precious in His sight.

Wouldest though give a stone, a serpent, to thy pleading child for food? And shall not thy Heavenly Father give thee what is good?

On the heart that careth for Thee, rest though then from sorrow free; For of all most tender fathers none so good as He.

Seek thou first His gracious promise, treasure stored in Heaven above; So thou mayest entrust all other safely to His love.

Reflection

17

From Life to Life

When I close my eyes, I see them lying there still and lifeless. This is hard to believe and difficult to comprehend. It's like yesterday and the pain starts again, like a knife cutting through me. It seems they are just around every corner; I'm looking for them to show up, waiting for them to return. Then, I close my eyes and see them lying there still and lifeless, and I'm helpless. I must remove that last visual, because that is not who they were. That is one moment in time, I will be intentional about visualizing the memories of who they were in life, not in earthly death, and imagine them in Glory. I will begin to see them in their new transformed life. That last visual was of what they left behind, the person I loved is no longer in that clay vessel, they have broken free. I know and believe they are forever with me now in my heart, everywhere I go. This is the truth.

Psalm 49:15 But God will redeem me from the realm of the dead; he will surely take me to himself.

John 5:24 Very truly I tell you, whoever hears my word and believes him who sent me has eternal life and will not be judged but has crossed over from death to life.

2 Corinthians 4:7 But we have this treasure in jars of clay to show that this all-surpassing power is from God and not from us.

1 Thessalonians 4:13-18 Brothers and sisters, we do not want you to be uninformed about those who sleep in death, so that you do not grieve like the rest of mankind, who have no hope. For we believe that Jesus died and rose again, and so we believe that God will bring with Jesus those who have fallen asleep in him. According to the Lord's word, we tell you that we who are still alive, who are left until the coming of the Lord, will certainly not precede those who have fallen asleep. For the Lord himself will come down from heaven, with a loud command, with the voice of the archangel and with the trumpet call of God, and the dead in Christ will rise first. After that, we who are still alive and are left will be caught up together with them in the clouds to meet the Lord in the air. And so we will be with the Lord forever. Therefore encourage one another with these words.

On the Resurrection Morning
(S. Baring-Gould)

On the resurrection morning, soul and body meet again, no more sorrow, no more weeping, no more pain.

Here awhile they must be parted and the flesh its sabbath keep, waiting in a holy stillness wrapt in sleep.

For a space that tired body lies with feet toward the dawn; till there breaks the last and brightest Easter morn.

But the soul in contemplation utters earnest prayers and strong'
breaking at the resurrection into song.

Soul and body reunited, thenceforth nothing will divide, waking up in
Christs own likeness, satisfied.

Oh, the beauty, oh, the gladness of that resurrection day! Which shall
not through endless ages, pass away!

On that happy Easter morning all the graves their dead restore, fa-
ther, sister, child and mother meet once more.

To that brightest of all meetings, bring us Jesus Christ, at last; to Thy
cross through death and judgment holding fast.

Reflection

18

He Restores My Soul

There are days where it feels like this will never get better. I pray, I say affirmations, I speak to others but still I hurt deeply in my inner most parts. That pain lingers each time I close my eyes and each time I open my eyes. I want to feel better now, but I don't and I'm not sure where to start. When I think of them, my very soul aches, I cry until I tremble. The Lord made us one and that part of me has gone back to Him. I feel this way today, but I'm determined not stay in this place. It's like a cut, with care new skin slowly begins from the inside out and one day it's complete. While a scar may remain the wound is healed, while I will never forget them the deepness of this pain will heal. I know and believe God's Word is true and I trust Him to renew me day by day. The Lord will restore my soul in the same way.

Psalm 23:2-3a (NKJV) He makes me to lie down in green pastures; He leads me beside the still waters. He restores my soul.

2 Corinthians 4:16-18 Therefore we do not lose heart. Though outwardly we are wasting away, yet inwardly we are being renewed day by day. For our light and momentary troubles are achieving for us an eternal glory that far outweighs them all. So we fix our eyes not on what is seen, but on what is unseen, since what is seen is temporary, but what is unseen is eternal.

Awake, our souls, away, our fears
(Isaac Watts)

Awake, our souls! Away, our fears! Let every trembling thought be gone! Awake, and run the heavenly race, and put a cheerful courage on.

True, 'tis a strait and thorny road, and mortal spirits tire and faint. But they forget the mighty God that feeds the strength of every saint.

The mighty God, Whose matchless power is ever young, and firm endures, while endless years their everlasting circles run.

From Thee, the ever-flowing spring, our souls shall drink a fresh supply; While such as trust their native strength shall melt away, and droop and die.

Swift as an eagle cuts the air, we'll mount aloft to Thine abode; On wings of love our soul shall fly, nor tire along the heavenly road.

Reflection

19

A Quiet Place

There is so much going on, and I must keep moving. The challenge is that although I would like to stop and reflect, subconsciously I don't want to stop as it would require facing the reality of their absence. I know I need to stop and consider everything that has happened, how I really feel, what I really think and listen to what the Lord has to say. I'm almost afraid of the feelings that will come out, but I must allow them, to begin to heal, to mourn. I know and believe the Lord will help me find a way to quiet my mind and spirit. My strength is in the Lord, and I desperately need to hear from Him. I can get up a few minutes earlier, go to sleep a few minutes later, take a little more time to say my grace, stay in the rest room, take a shower, or walk the dog and use those extra minutes to reflect, pray and listen. I will find my quiet place so I can hear my thoughts and hear God.

Psalm 62:5 (EHV) My soul, rest quietly in God alone, for my hope comes from him.

Mark 1:35 Very early in the morning, while it was still dark, Jesus got up, left the house and went off to a solitary place, where he prayed.

Mark 6:31 Then, because so many people were coming and going that they did not even have a chance to eat, he said to them, "Come with me by yourselves to a quiet place and get some rest."

Guide Me O Thou Great Jehovah
(William Williams)

Guide me, O Thou great Jehovah, pilgrim through this barren land; I am weak, but Thou art mighty, hold me with Thy powerful hand; Bread of heaven, Bread of heaven, feed me now and evermore.

Open now the crystal fountain, Whence the healing streams do flow; Let the fiery cloudy pillar lead me all my journey through. Strong Deliverer, Strong Deliverer, be Thou still my Strength and Shield.

When I tread the verge of Jordan, bid my anxious fears subside; Death of death and hell's destruction, land me safe on Canaan's side. Songs of praises, Songs of praises, I will ever give to thee.

Reflection

20

All the Personal Items

It is so difficult to straighten the dresser, open the closet, handle the last set of laundry, move that favorite cup or their toothbrush. All the memories and reminders that they were here but are no longer here. I want them to stay where they were and how they were so my heart can be warmed by them. The personal items keep them close to me, but each time I see them, smell them, touch them and savor those precious moments we shared, I can smile inside while also feeling the pain again. I know I must release these, as I've released them to the Lord, but it's difficult. Each time I try, it feels like I'm throwing away a piece of them that I should keep. I must allow the Lord to help me work through this painful step. I know and believe the Lord will strengthen me. If I must do it with only the Lord I will, but if a family member or friend is available, I'll ask them to join me. I must move forward, albeit slowly, but forward. I'll touch the items, smell them and hold them. I'll cry and sit with them. I'll say a prayer and release them. Those that are especially sentimental, I'll keep, but the rest, I'll release. Getting through the first batch will be the hardest, but with God's help I'll do it.

Psalm 34:4–5 & 8 I sought the Lord, and he answered me; he delivered me from all my fears. Those who look to him are radiant; their faces are never covered with shame. Taste and see that the Lord is good; blessed is the one who takes refuge in him.

Philippians 4:13 (NKJV) I can do all things through Christ who strengthens me.

Isaiah 41:13 For I am the Lord your God who takes hold of your right hand and says to you, Do not fear, I will help you.

Just As I Am Without One Plea
(Charlotte Elliott)

Just as I am without one plea, but that Thy Blood was shed for me, and that Thou biddest me come to Thee, O Lamb of God, I come.

Just as I am, though tossed about with many a conflict, many a doubt, Fightings and fears within, without, O Lamb of God, I come.

Just as I am, poor, wretched, blind; sight, riches, healing of the mind, yea all I need, in Thee to find, O Lamb of God, I come.

Just as I am, Thou wilt receive, wilt welcome pardon, cleanse relieve, Because Thy promise I believe, O Lamb of God, I come.

Just as I am, Thy love unknown has broken every barrier down. Now to Thine, yea, Thine alone, O Lamb of God I come.

Just as I am, of that free love, the breadth, length, depth and height to prove, here for a season then above O Lamb of God, I come.

Reflection

21

Am I Being Selfish?

The pain I feel, they don't have. I cry, I grieve, I ache without them, but they are fine with Christ. The pain is like a sharp knife in my stomach, but as I move my thoughts from my pain, to thinking of them and of Christ I can smile through the tears. Maybe its selfish that I haven't considered they have reached the destination they longed for, the place for which I also long after walking my Christian journey. I know and believe eternity with Jesus is the goal, they've just gone ahead of me. So, through the pain, I can also feel their joy and rejoice in that glorious hope. I open my hand and open my heart and release them to the Lord they loved. I'm fully confident they are at peace awaiting the resurrection, and I will meet them again.

Psalm 116:15 Precious in the sight of the Lord is the death of his faithful servants.

Philippians 1:21 For to me, to live is Christ and to die is gain.

1 Corinthians 15:54-55 When the perishable has been clothed with the imperishable, and the mortal with immortality, then the saying that is written will come true: 'Death has been swallowed up in victory. 'Where, O death, is your victory? Where, O death, is your sting?'

Romans 15:13 May the God of hope fill you with all joy and peace as you trust in Him, so that you may overflow with hope by the power of the Holy Spirit.

The Saints in Glory
(Isaac Watts)

Give us the wings of faith to rise within the veil, and see the Saints above, how great their joys, how bright their glories be.

Once they were mourning here below, and wet their couch with tears; they wrestled hard, as we do now, with sins and doubts and fears.

We ask them whence their victory came; they, with united breath, ascribe their conquest to the Lamb, their triumph to His death.

They marked the footsteps that He trod, His zeal inspired their breast, and, following their incarnate God, they reached the promised rest.

Our glorious Leader claims our praise, for His own pattern given; while the great cloud of witnesses show the same path to heaven.

Reflection

22

It's Okay to Not Be Okay

Every day and several times a day, someone asks 'How are you? I'm checking on you." I know they are well intentioned, but my spouse has transitioned, I'm not okay. My life has changed forever, everything I've known in the past has changed and will never be the same. They also don't really want to know how I'm doing, it's a rhetorical question. I don't want to share my deepest feelings with everyone, so I say I'm okay and keep going. In fact, some days and parts of days are better than others. I never know when a memory will make me smile or cry at an instant. Part of me is gone, I am not okay. All I can do is hold on to God and memories. In time, with God's help, I won't cry so much, the sharpness of the pain will reduce, and I'll truly smile again from within. For now, I'll trust God from day to day, I'll get something to keep with me all the time to remember them. It may be something of theirs or something new, but whenever I touch it or look at it, I acknowledge that I'm mourning and it's okay not to be okay. I trust and believe God with the process.

Psalm 71:20-21 Though you have made me see troubles, many and bitter, you will restore my life again; from the depths of the earth you will again bring me up. You will increase my honor and comfort me once more.

Matthew 5:4 Blessed are those who mourn, for they will be comforted.

John 11:35 Jesus wept.

Hebrews 4:15-16 For we do not have a high priest who is unable to empathize with our weaknesses, but we have one who has been tempted in every way, just as we are—yet he did not sin. Let us then approach God's throne of grace with confidence, so that we may receive mercy and find grace to help us in our time of need.

Fight the Good Fight
(John S. B. Monsell)

Fight the good fight with all thy might, Christ is thy strength and Christ thy right. Lay hold on life and it shall be, thy joy and crown eternally.

Run the straight race through God's good grace; lift up thine eyes and seek his face. Life with its way before us lies; Christ is the path and Christ the prize.

Cast care aside, lean on thy Guide; His boundless mercy will provide. Trust and thy trusting soul shall prove, Christ is its life and Christ its love.

Faint not, nor fear, His arms are near; He changeth not, and thou art dear. Only believe, and thou shalt see that Christ is all in all to thee.

Reflection

23

Others Can Help Me

I'm a Christian and love the Lord, but I can't think, I can't pray, I can't focus, I'm just going through the motions or what is necessary each day. There is a void and I feel like I should just read my scriptures and it will be okay. I've done all I know to do and it hasn't gotten better. There are others who have been through this and understand. I know and believe the Lord has Christian professionals who are counselors, therapist and psychiatrists who can help. I will reach out to someone, because the enemy wants me to stay in a dark place, with a sub-standard faith walk. I will not stay in this place, and I don't have to do this alone. I will move forward and get the help I need.

Psalm 73:24 You guide me with your counsel, and afterward you will take me into glory.

Proverbs 15:22 Plans fail for lack of counsel, but with many advisers they succeed.

Proverbs 19:20 (NKJV) Listen to counsel and receive instruction, That you may be wise in your latter days.

1 Thessalonians 5:11 Therefore encourage one another and build one another up, just as you are doing.

God of Our Life to Thee We Call
(William Cowper)

God of our life, to Thee we call, afflicted at Thy feet we fall; When the great water-floods prevail, leave not our trembling hearts to fail.

Friend of the friendless and the faint, where should we lodge our deep complaint? Where but with Thee, whose open door, invites the help-less and the poor?

Did ever mourner plead with Thee, and Thou refuse that mourner's plea? Does not the Word still fixed remain, that none shall seek Thy face in vain?

Then hear, O Lord, our humble cry, and bend on us Thy pitying eye; To Thee their prayer Thy people make, hear us for our Redeemer's sake.

Reflection

24

Moving On and Moving Forward Are Different

Each time someone says, "It's okay, just move on." I give half a smile, for their sake, and nod, because they have no idea what is happening inside me. Just hearing that, hurts. There is no such thing as moving on, that implies leaving their memories in the past and going to the next person, or thing in my life as if they were never there. This is not possible and it's also not what I want. Moving on would not honor them and their place in my life. I want to honor their memory and keep them close. They are a part of all that I am today, my future will be influenced by them having been an integral part of my life. Embracing all they are and have been to me, allows me to take them along and move forward in full self-awareness of who I am, while not stuck in the past. I take the time I need to sit with my grief, mourn their departure and adjust to a life without them physically present, while working on healing and allowing the Lord to show me the next step in my life. I will not move on, but I know and believe I can and will move forward with God's help.

Psalm 125:1-2 Those who trust in the Lord are like Mount Zion, which cannot be shaken but endures forever. As the mountains surround Jerusalem, so the Lord surrounds his people both now and forevermore.

Jeremiah 29:11 "For I know the plans I have for you," declares the Lord, "plans to prosper you and not to harm you, plans to give you hope and a future."

Philippians 3:12-14 (MSG) I'm not saying that I have this all together, that I have it made. But I am well on my way, reaching out for Christ, who has so wondrously reached out for me. Friends, don't get me wrong: By no means do I count myself an expert in all of this, but I've got my eye on the goal, where God is beckoning us onward—to Jesus. I'm off and running, and I'm not turning back.

Higher Ground
(Johnson Oatman, Jr.)

I'm pressing on the upward way, new heights I'm gaining every day; still praying as I'm onward bound, "Lord plant my feet on higher ground."

My heart has no desire to stay where doubts arise and fears dismay; Though some may dwell where these abound, my prayer, my aim, is higher ground.

I want to live above the world, though Satan's darts at me are hurled; for faith has caught a joyful sound, the song of saints on higher ground.

I want to scale the utmost height and catch a gleam of glory bright; but still I'll pray till heaven I've found, "Lord lead me on to higher ground."

Lord, lift me up, and let me stand by faith, on heaven's tableland; a higher plane than I have found, Lord plant my feet on higher ground.

Reflection

25

Things Left Undone

Everything happened so fast. We were just starting, we were in the middle of doing so much, we were planning for the next chapter in our life and now they are gone. Suddenly, gone, with no advance warning or time to prepare. We planned to talk about many things, but never did. I don't know what to do next, or even know where everything is in the process. We talked about some things. We talked about nothing. So many things are left undone, and I can't pick up where they left off. This is out of my control; I will put my trust in the Lord, He knows what happened and that I need help. I know and believe He has not left me alone with all these things left undone, I trust Him and will look to Him alone for guidance.

Psalm 32:8 I will instruct you and teach you in the way you should go; I will counsel you with my loving eye on you.

Proverbs 3:5-6 Trust in the Lord with all your heart and lean not on your own understanding; in all your ways submit to him, and he will make your paths straight.

Matthew 6:8 For your Father knows what you need before you ask him.

Put Thou Thy Trust in God
(Paul Gerhardt)

Put thou thy trust in God, In duty's path go on; Walk in His strength with faith and hope, so shall thy work be done.

Commit thy ways to Him, Thy works into His hands, and rest on His unchanging word, who heaven and earth commands.

Though years on years roll on His covenant shall endure, though clouds and darkness hide His path the promised grace is sure.

Give to the winds thy fears; Hope and be undismayed; God hears thy sighs and counts thy tears, God shall lift up thy head.

Through waves, and clouds, and storms, His power will clear thy way, Wait thou His time, the darkest night shall end in brightest day.

Leave to His sovereign sway to choose and to command; so shalt thou, wondering, own His way, How wise, how strong His hand.

Reflection

26

Even Christians Must Grieve

I know they are where they always wanted to be, with the God they loved. I know they have no more worries, tears, pain, or concerns. I know they love me and our family and would have stayed if they could. I know they were ready for eternal life with Jesus, and I know they are in a better place. Knowing all this, I still feel like there is a weight holding me down. I love the Lord, but there is no bypassing the grieving process, I am human. I know Jesus gave himself some time to grieve and pray when his cousin John the Baptist was killed, and he also wept when his friend Lazarus died. I will give myself some grace and allow myself to go through the process of grief and mourning.

Psalm 34:18 The Lord is close to the brokenhearted and saves those who are crushed in spirit.

Matthew 14:12-13 John's disciples came and took his body and buried it. Then they went and told Jesus. When Jesus heard what had happened, he withdrew by boat privately to a solitary place.

John 11:33-35 When Jesus saw her weeping, and the Jews who had come along with her also weeping, he was deeply moved in spirit and troubled. "Where have you laid him?" he asked. "Come and see, Lord," they replied. Jesus wept.

Ecclesiastes 3:1 and 4 There is a time for everything, and a season for every activity under the heavens: A time to weep and a time to laugh, a time to mourn and a time to dance.

Matthew 5:4 Blessed are those who mourn, for they will be comforted.

O Let Him Whose Sorrow No Relief Can Find
(Heinrich S. Oswald)

O let him, whose sorrow no relief can find, trust in God, and borrow ease for heart and mind.

When the mourner weeping, sheds the secret tear, God His watch is keeping, though none else be near.

God will never leave thee, all thy wants He knows, feels the pains that grieve thee, sees thy cares and woes.

Raise thine eyes to Heaven, when thy spirits quail, when by tempests driven, heart and courage fail.

When in grief we languish, He will dry the tear, Who His children's anguish soothes with succor near.

All our woe and sadness, in this world below, balance not the gladness we in Heaven shall know.

Jesus, Holy Savior, in the realms above, crown us with Thy favor, fill us with thy love.

Reflection

27

I Feel Lonely

I'm lonely. I have no one to talk to, no one with whom to share a laugh or take a walk. No one to share a meal with me. I wake up and they are not here, I go through the day, they are not here, I go to sleep they are not here. I'm alone and lonely. My mind is always on the things I miss and that companionship of being with someone, even when no words are spoken. The television helps sometimes, but it is not a real companion. I'm not interested in anything or anyone. I just want to be with them. I know the Lord loves me and doesn't want me to think like this. I need the help of the Holy Spirit because I can only see darkness and feel loneliness. This is a difficult and dark place. I prefer my memories over engaging with people. As difficult as it may be, I will focus on Jesus, others, and happy memories. My human need for companionship and interaction can be fulfilled through service, involvement in my community, outside exercise, looking out the window at God's awesome nature, or just calling friends. I can sit in the stillness, talk to Jesus, and feel the presence of the Holy Spirit. Occupying my mind will remove the feeling of loneliness. I know and believe Jesus is my constant companion and will bring people around when I need more.

Psalm 147:3 He heals the brokenhearted and binds up their wounds.

Psalm 55:16-17 As for me, I call to God, and the Lord saves me. Evening, morning and noon I cry out in distress, and he hears my voice.

John 14:16-17 (KJV) And I will pray the Father, and he shall give you another Comforter, that he may abide with you for ever; Even the Spirit of truth; whom the world cannot receive, because it seeth him not, neither knoweth him: but ye know him; for he dwelleth with you, and shall be in you.

Be Still, My Soul
(Kathrina von Schlegel)

Be still, my soul; the Lord is on thy side; bear patiently the cross of grief or pain. Leave to thy God to order and provide; in every change He faithful will remain. Be still, my soul; thy best, thy heavenly Friend through thorny ways leads to a joyful end.

Be still, my soul; thy God doth undertake to guide the future as He has the past. Thy hope, thy confidence let nothing shake; all now mysterious shall be bright at last. Be still, my soul; the waves and winds still know His voice who ruled them while He dwelt below.

Be still, my soul; when dearest friends depart, and all is darkened in the veil of tears, then shalt thou better know His love, His heart, who comes to soothe thy sorrow and thy fears.

Be still, my soul; thy Jesus can repay from His own fullness all He takes away.

Reflection

28

A New Normal

Life as I knew it has changed. I go about the day doing many of the things I've always done, interacting with family, friends, work, and social events. But I'm not fully present in any of these. There is a void in my life. My normal has changed. I feel disorientated going through life without them. The house is empty without them, there is no one to laugh with or discuss family and life issues, when the bedroom door closes, it's only me in the room. This is my new normal and I must embrace it. I will give each day, and myself, to the Lord and intentionally allow time to adjust. Major changes in any area take time, so does this. No matter how long it takes, I will continue to seek the Lord's face until my change comes. I know that one day I will get through a day without crying and the pain will not feel so sharp, but it may not be soon. It doesn't matter if others were better sooner; I am not them. I know and believe that if I am honest with the Lord, He will help me day by day. I embrace each day and stay in the present. How I handle the issues of the day may be new, but with the Lord's help, I will conquer my fears and uncertainty to move forward. I will deliberately take the time I need to work on myself as I stay aware of the adjustments to my new reality.

Psalm 105:4 Look to the Lord and his strength; seek his face always.

Job 14:14 (KJV) All the days of my appointed time will I wait, till my change come.

Isaiah 54:10 Though the mountains be shaken and the hills be removed, yet my unfailing love for you will not be shaken nor my covenant of peace be removed," says the Lord, who has compassion on you.

Habakkuk 2:3 For the revelation awaits an appointed time; it speaks of the end and will not prove false. Though it linger, wait for it; it will certainly come and will not delay.

God Is Working His Purpose Out
(Arthur Campbell Ainger)

God is working his purpose out, as year succeeds to year; God is working his purpose out, and the time is drawing near; nearer and near draws the time, the time that shall surely be; when the earth shall be filled with the glory of God as the waters cover the sea.

From utmost east to utmost west, where human feet have trod, by the mouth of many messengers goes forth the voice of God; 'Give ear to me, ye continents, yes isles, give ear to me, that the earth may be filled with the glory of God as the waters cover the sea."

Let us go forth in the strength of God, with the banner of Christ unfurled, that the light of the glorious gospel of truth may shine throughout the world. Let us all fight with sorrow and sin to set the captives free, that the earth may be filled with the glory of God as the waters cover the sea.

All we can do is nothing worth unless God blesses the deed. Vainly we hope for the harvest-tide till God gives life to the seed. Yet nearer and nearer draws the time, the time that shall surely be, when the earth shall be filled with the glory of God as the waters cover the sea.

Reflection

.

29

The Marriage Mystery

I miss them in so many ways. Our marriage gave us the intimacy of a couple and I miss that. That mystery of marriage, of two becoming one was created by God. That intimacy which was integral to the sacrament of marriage is now gone and I crave it, but I don't know how to handle the feelings. All of this is so new, I want to do the right thing, the desires are real. Lord, help me with this, you know about this too. No one talks about this, but it was a part of my married life and it's also gone. I must address this, too, with God's help. When I begin to have those desires and feelings, I release them to God. I need the Lord to help me through those moments and protect me from myself. If I follow those desires, I become vulnerable to emotions that lead to a place I should not be. This is difficult, but I trust and believe you Jesus. Lord, you know everything about me. I will wait for you.

Psalm 139:1-4 You have searched me, Lord, and you know me. You know when I sit and when I rise; you perceive my thoughts from afar. You discern my going out and my lying down; you are familiar with all my ways. Before a word is on my tongue you, Lord, know it completely.

Psalm 119:9 How can a young person stay on the path of purity? By living according to your word.

Matthew 19:6 So they are no longer two, but one flesh. Therefore, what God has joined together, let no one separate.

1 Corinthians 7:8-9 Now to the unmarried and the widows I say: It is good for them to stay unmarried, as I do. But if they cannot control themselves, they should marry, for it is better to marry than to burn with passion.

All to Jesus I Surrender
(Judson W. Van DeVenter)

All to Jesus I surrender, All to Him I freely give; I will ever love and trust Him, In His presence daily live.

All to Jesus I surrender, Humbly at His feet I bow, Worldly pleasures all forsaken; Take me, Jesus, take me now.

All to Jesus I surrender, Make me, Savior, wholly Thine; Let me feel Thy Holy Spirit, Truly know that Thou art mine.

All to Jesus I surrender, Lord, I give myself to Thee; Fill me with Thy love and power, Let Thy blessing fall on me.

All to Jesus I surrender, now I feel the sacred flame. Oh, the joy of full salvation! Glory, glory to His name.

I surrender all, I surrender all. All to Thee, my blessed Savior, I surrender all.

Reflection

30

Death Has Parted Us

The traditional marriage vows were till death do us part. Even if we said non-traditional vows, it was our intention to stay together for life's full journey. The commitment made before God and others has been honored. For that I'm grateful. Marriage wasn't always easy, but staying was worth it. Now I'm a widow(er). I never thought this would come, but here I am. What we had was so special, I can't imagine loving again, allowing my heart to be vulnerable again. Just moving their clothes seems like a betrayal. If I love another, I'd need to move their photos and all the good memories, to bring someone in. I'm not sure I can do that, I don't want to do that. Maybe I will try to open my heart again, maybe I'm comfortable going the rest of the journey without a life companion. Whatever I decide, there is no guilt, I honored the marriage commitment. I know and believe the Lord will guide my heart. If I venture into a new relationship, I must be emotionally and spiritually ready. I will stay before the Lord, adjust to my new normal, embrace the present, learn something new, protect my heart and emotions, take major decisions slowly, and give myself lots of time to grieve, mourn, and heal from the transition of my love.

Psalm 40:1-3 I waited patiently for the Lord; he turned to me and heard my cry. He lifted me out of the slimy pit, out of the mud and mire; he set my feet on a rock and gave me a firm place to stand. He put a new song in my mouth, a hymn of praise to our God. Many will see and fear the Lord and put their trust in him.

Psalm 30:5 Weeping may stay for the night, but rejoicing comes in the morning.

1 Corinthians 7:39 A woman is bound to her husband as long as he lives. But if her husband dies, she is free to marry anyone she wishes, but he must belong to the Lord.

Ephesians 3:16-19 I pray that out of his glorious riches he may strengthen you with power through his Spirit in your inner being, so that Christ may dwell in your hearts through faith. And I pray that you, being rooted and established in love, may have power, together with all the Lord's holy people, to grasp how wide and long and high and deep is the love of Christ, and to know this love that surpasses knowledge—that you may be filled to the measure of all the fullness of God.

Isaiah 61:2b and 3 To comfort all who mourn and provide for those who grieve in Zion—to bestow on them a crown of beauty instead of ashes, the oil of joy instead of mourning, and a garment of praise instead of a spirit of despair. They will be called oaks of righteousness, a planting of the Lord for the display of his splendor.

For All the Saints
(William Walsham How)

For all the saints who from their labors rest, who Thee by faith before the world confessed; Thy name, O Jesus, be forever blest. Alleluia, Alleluia!

Thou wast their Rock, their Fortress and their Might; Thou, Lord, their Captain in the well-fought fight; Thou, in the darkness drear, their one true Light. Alleluia, Alleluia!

O may Thy soldiers, faithful, true and bold, Fight as the Saints who nobly fought of old, And win with them, the victor's crown of gold. Alleluia, Alleluia!

O blest communion, fellowship divine! We feebly struggle, they in glory shine; yet all are one in Thee, for all are Thine. Alleluia, Alleluia!

And when the strife is fierce, the warfare long, steals on the ear the distant triumph song, and hearts are brave again, and arms are strong. Alleluia, Alleluia!

The golden evening brightens in the west; soon, soon to faithful warriors comes their rest; sweet is the calm of Paradise the blest. Alleluia, Alleluia!

But lo! there breaks a yet more glorious day: the Saints triumphant rise in bright array; the King of glory passes on His way. Alleluia, Alleluia!

From earth's wide bounds, from ocean's farthest coast, through gates of pearl streams in the countless host, singing to Father, Son, and Holy Ghost. Alleluia, Alleluia!

Reflection

When Will It Get Better

The Edge of Grief: A Summer Reflection
(By Ellen Frankel LCSW)

"Will it ever stop hurting so much? Will we ever get over the grief?

These were the questions being put on the table by participants in a support group I was facilitating for those who were recently bereaved. They debated the often-cited notion that time heals all wounds, for the wounds they brought into that room were large, deep gashes, raw and oozing and too tender to touch. It was nearly impossible for most of those present that night to imagine a time when the pain would ever be bearable. There was "before" and now there was "after." The death of their loved one turned their hearts inside out, and their lives upside down.

As a bereavement counselor, it is my job to help create a safe space to give voice to the unspeakable, and to companion others in their grief journey as they travel into the wilderness of their soul in search of their own inner knowing and truth.

But it's a messy business, this grief work. There is no GPS saying where to turn, or when to recalculate, or when you will ever arrive at your destination.

One man asked, "Does it ever go away, this pain? Do we ever really heal after losing someone we loved?"

His question resonated with the group members and they began discussing and exploring with one another. One woman, whose mother died a couple of months prior asked another member who had lost her loved one nearly a year ago if the grief changes at all, and if so, how? While they talked, I listened. Then a group member turned to me and asked, "What do you think? Do we ever get over the pain of our loss? Does the grief ever end?"

I waited a moment, thinking how I wanted to respond as their group facilitator, but before I could get the words out of my head, my broken heart answered from its own truth instead. The words came from my heart as a daughter whose father had died a year ago, and as I spoke them, I heard them for the first time.

This is what I told them:

> When you break a glass on the kitchen floor, you have to be careful when you go to clean up. The glass is sharp—so very sharp—so as you pick it up, piece by piece, you have to go slowly, touch the glass cautiously, because even the slightest encounter with the edge can pierce your skin and you hurt and you bleed. The

shards of glass are harsh and the edges cut deeply. Now imagine that those broken pieces of glass have been thrown into the ocean. They are at the mercy of the current, and have to let go into the forces of nature. Some days, the ocean roars with big forceful waves and the glass is tossed and churned and thrown along with the rocks and sand. Other times, the ocean is gentle, and the glass is stroked by the rhythm of the tide. Yet just as the gentle ocean lulls the glass with its soothing melody, another storm hits and the glass is once again pushed against the force of currents, the force of the moon and the heavens. And yet again, at some point the ocean quiets, the flow is once again soft, the waves flow like the inhalation and exhalation of the breath, arriving at the shore, hugging the sand.

And at some point, there you are, on a warm, sunny July day, walking along the seashore when you stop because just in front of you, sitting amidst pebbles and rocks and periwinkle shells is a piece of sea glass. You bend down to pick it up, marveling at your good fortune to find this treasure. Holding it in your hands you feel its smoothness and the places where the sea glass might have a slight ridge. You can rub it on all of its sides, for no longer are there sharp edges. Instead, the edges have become solid and smooth and you can hold it tightly in your hand without fear of injury. In fact, holding it in your hand feels fortifying and strengthening. We actively seek these brilliant pieces of sea glass precisely because they echo the beauty of survival, of resiliency, and of hope.

With tenderness and love you are able to hold this piece of sea glass and learn its unique features. Where once the edges of the glass were jagged and sharp, now the edges are ever softly rounded, so that you can run a finger over them repeatedly, and it will not take your blood.

That is how grief can change, I told the group members. Those are the edges of grief.

Menachem Mendel of Kotzk, the great Chassidic rebbe said, 'Nothing is as whole as a broken heart.' I think that is why so many people on the beach, children and adults alike, feel that finding sea glass is like finding a treasure. When we hold a piece of sea glass, we hold in our hands what was once part of something broken, something that was sharp and painful to the touch. When we hold it after its time of being housed in the ocean of life, it becomes stronger in the broken places and each small piece we find tells us that we too, are a treasure. We too can grow stronger from our grief. A friend of mine, who lost three family members within a two-year period, told me that each loss has made her a kinder person. Each loss has made her softer at the edges.

I looked into the faces of the group members, and we all took a moment to look at one another and breathe. Our broken hearts understood this in a way that allowed us to look at the gnawing gash of our wounds and understand that even in our pain, healing had already begun. Even in our most piercing and painful moments, the edges of grief are touching the forces of nature, the ebbs and the flows, and in its own time, there would be a grief that we could hold as a treasure of love, of memories, of beauty and connection.

Reflection

www.ingramcontent.com/pod-product-compliance
Lightning Source LLC
Chambersburg PA
CBHW032002080426
42735CB00007B/483